THE SPIRITUAL WARFARE DEVOTIONAL PRAYER BOOK FOR BEGINNERS

PRAYERS YOU NEED TO KNOW TO FIGHT THE WILES OF THE DEVIL

Virginia A. Lewis

Copyright © 2021 Virginia A. Lewis

All rights reserved

No part of this book may be reproduced, or stored in a retrieval system, or transmitted in any form or by any means, electronic, mechanical, photocopying, recording, or otherwise, without express written permission of the publisher.

Portion of this text may be reprinted for use in small groups, church bulletins, order of services, Sunday school lessons, church newsletters, and similar works, in the course of religious instructions, or services at a place of worship or other religious assembly with the following notices attached:
SPIRITUAL WARFARE DEVOTIONAL PRAYER BOOK FOR BEGINNER
by: Virginia A. Lewis

If you purchased this book without a cover, you should be aware that this book is stolen property. It has been reported as "unsold and destroyed" to the author and publisher, and neither party has received any payment for this "stripped" book.

works cited:
Erickson, M. (2016, June 2). The Truth About Spiritual Warfare and Why It's Important to Pray. Retrieved April 22, 2021, from https://www.lifeway.com/en/articles/are-you-fighting-a-spiritual-war-priscilla-shirer-armor-of-god

Munguti, J. (2016, September 13). 8 Functions of the Holy Spirit as Taught by Jesus. Retrieved April 22, 2021, from https://www.christiantruthcenter.com/functions-of-the-holy-spirit/

John 16:13 However, when he, the Spirit of truth, is come, he will guide you into all truth: for he shall not speak of himself; but whatever he shall hear, that shall he speak: and he will show you things to come. (n.d.). Retrieved April 22, 2021, from https://bibleapps.com/commentaries/john/16-13.htm

Erickson, M. (2016, June 2). The Truth About Spiritual Warfare and Why It's Important to Pray. Retrieved April 22, 2021, from https://www.lifeway.com/en/articles/are-you-fighting-a-spiritual-war-priscilla-shirer-armor-of-god

Dictionary by Merriam-Webster: America's most-trusted online dictionary. (2021, April 24). Retrieved April 24, 2021, from https://www.merriam-webster.com

Scriptures taken from:
NEW KING JAMES BIBLE ONLINE WEBSITE! (n.d.). Retrieved April 23, 2021, from https://www.kingjamesbibleonline.org/new-features.php

ESV.org. (n.d.). Retrieved April 23, 2021, from https://www.esv.org/

Products - NIV Bibles. (n.d.). Retrieved April 23, 2021, from https://www.thenivbible.com/products/

Cover design by: Slonelynn Gigs
Printed in the United States of America

CONTENTS

Title Page
Copyright
Introduction · 1
1. The Truth about Spiritual Warfare
2. How to Pray Through Spiritual Warfare
3. Spiritual Warfare and the Devil
4. The Holy Spirit in Spiritual War
5. Prayer for Spiritual Warfare
6. A Prayer for Cover Against Evil
A Prayer to protect Against Spiritual Attacks · 11
Prayer for cover from the Wiles of the Devil · 12
7. How to Have a Personal Christian Devotion
8. How are You Involved in Spiritual Warfare?
9. Fighting the Spiritual Battle as Jesus Did
10. How to Prepare for Spiritual Warfare · 19
11. Seasoned Believers
12. Spiritual Warfare for each Believer
13. Six Spiritual Seasons of Life · 25
14. A Prayer for When Enemies Strike · 29
15. Eight Functions of the Holy Spirit, as Taught by Jesus · 30
Virginia's Message to Her Readers · 32
About The Author · 33

INTRODUCTION

What is spiritual warfare? In the Bible, spiritual warfare is when a Christian fights against the work of the enemy of God, the devil.

The elements of God's armor against the enemy are described in Ephesians 6: 10-17. There are seven pieces of armor described here.

Christian author and speaker Priscilla Shirer says of this passage of Scripture, "When Paul speaks of spiritual war in Ephesians 6, prayer is the seventh piece of armor. It activates all of the remainders of the spiritual armor," When we refuse to pray, it is like having a refrigerator without plugging it in. Prayer is the divinely authorized mechanism God has given us to tap into his power. Without prayer, we will be ineffective in spiritual warfare; with it, we will be victorious."

✼ ✼ ✼

1. THE TRUTH ABOUT SPIRITUAL WARFARE

Shirer says that everything that happens within the visible and physical world is directly connected to the battle that is being waged in the invisible, unseen world. "The effects of the war being fought within the unseen world reveal themselves in our strained and damaged relationships, emotional instability, mental fatigue, physical exhaustion, and lots of other areas of life. Many folks feel pinned down by anger, unforgiveness, pride, comparisons, insecurity, discord, fear--the list goes on. The primary spiritual nemesis we have is the devil himself."

Ephesians 6:12 says: "For we do not wrestle against flesh and blood, but against the principalities, against powers, against the rulers of the darkness of this age, against spiritual hosts of wickedness in the heavenly places." (NKJV)

Craving and Praying for Spiritual Vision

We need spiritual vision to understand who we are in Christ. Shirer tells us that God has already given us everything we need to win the spiritual battles we face. It is through prayer that we recognize and use the spiritual warfare weapons described in Ephesians 6.

Shirer says we should always ask the Lord to open our eyes to be aware of the enemy's activity and be more conscious of the spiritual resources He has given us to disarm and defeat him. Victory is available for us, but it will only come if we pray for God's help.

2. HOW TO PRAY THROUGH SPIRITUAL WARFARE

Spiritual warfare is a term that Christians use, but many Christians do not fully understand what it is, and how to fight this warfare.

Spiritual warfare can be compared to physical warfare. Historical battles are often about controlling areas for political or economic power. Spiritual Warfare is the battle for control over people's souls.

Whether we believe in Him or not, God created us for a reason. He created us to understand Him and His love. He created us to love others as we love ourselves and use our skills and talents for the good of the planet — to point people to Him.

However, God has an enemy. His name is Satan, or the Devil. Because he is the enemy of God and God's people, he has sometimes been called a "villain."

Satan is committed to preventing people from knowing God and trusting him with their lives. The Enemy's tactics vary depending on whether someone is a Christian or not, but his main goal is to keep people from experiencing the love of God.

❋ ❋ ❋

3. SPIRITUAL WARFARE AND THE DEVIL

The devil has been defeated by what Jesus accomplished when He died on the cross. Jesus' resurrection from the dead shows His triumph over death. But the devil wants to blind people to this truth.

The devil's attempts to send us astray in our relationship with God go back to the beginning of human history.

We all know the story of Adam and Eve's temptation. In Genesis chapter 3 we get a picture of the character of Satan:

- ❖ He is more cunning than a wild animal.
- ❖ He pretends to be our ally.
- ❖ He seeks to create doubts in our minds about what God says.
- ❖ He wants us to believe God places undue restrictions on us.
- ❖ He tempts us to rebel against God by showing us that we can be the ruler of our own lives.
- ❖ He appeals to our pride to get us to do his will.

Note that our enemy, the devil, is a real being. He is cunning and dangerous; it's not wise to try to fight him alone. But we don't need to fight him alone, because we as believers have the Holy Spirit within us.

4. THE HOLY SPIRIT IN SPIRITUAL WAR

There is one God, with three persons in the godhead: The Father, the Son, and the Holy Spirit. The Holy Spirit is the most misunderstood person of the Trinity. To experience a consistent victory in a spiritual war, it is essential to understand the role of the Holy Spirit in our lives.

After Jesus rose from the dead, He appeared to His disciples. They were scared and confused. They did not yet have the power of the Holy Spirit within them.

Jesus wanted His followers to have the strength to fight their spiritual battles. So, he told them that the source of their greatest strength, the Holy Spirit, would now live within them: John 20:21-22 says, "'Peace be with you! Because the Father has sent Me, I am sending you.' And thereupon He breathed on them and said, 'Receive the Holy Spirit"

God is a being superior to man. But Jesus, the second Person of the Trinity, became a man. He experienced the same struggles and hardships that we as humans experience, even though he was God. When he returned to the Father, His presence on earth was replaced by the Holy Spirit's presence.

So, as we experience spiritual warfare, we are not relying on our own strength, or even the strength that God gives us through prayer and reading His Word. We literally have God within us, in the form of the Holy Spirit.

Scriptures that assist you in praying Through Spiritual Warfare.

Try praying the following Bible verses when you are engaged in spiritual battles. Insert your own name or the name of a person you are praying for into the text.

2 Corinthians 10:3-5 (NIV)

"For though we live in the world, we do not wage war as the world does. The weapons we fight with are not the weapons of the world. On the contrary, they have divine power to demolish strongholds. We demolish arguments and every pretension that sets itself up against the knowledge of God, and we take captive every thought to make it obedient to Christ."

Isaiah 54:17 (NIV)

"'No weapon forged against you will prevail, and you will refute every tongue that accuses you. This is the heritage of the servants of the LORD, and this is their vindication from me,' declares the LORD."

John 8:32 (NIV)

"Then you will know the truth, and the truth will set you free."

1 Peter 5:7 (NIV)

"Cast all your anxiety on Him because He cares for you."

John 15: 7 (NIV)

"If you remain in Me and My words remain in you, ask whatever you wish, and it will be done for you."

Spiritual Warfare: Understanding the Battle

To understand the battle of spiritual warfare, we need to acknowledge that we are in a war. A war is made up of a series of battles fought in different locations. The dictionary definition of battle is, "combat between persons, between factions, between armies. Any type of extended contest, struggle, or controversy." As Christians, we are always in a spiritual battle of some sort. If we aren't in a spiritual battle, that means we're already in heaven. Battles are waged on various fronts, for different reasons, and with varying degrees of intensity. This is true also for spiritual warfare. Our spiritual battles are real, even though we cannot physically see the enemy. We can discuss how the battles are fought and how they impact our lives from day to day.

You may be asking yourself, "Why should I even want to engage in a spiritual battle?" There is no hope for us to succeed in spiritual battle if we don't know what we are fighting for.

In spiritual warfare, we are either victors or victims. Jesus already conquered the enemy when He died and rose from the dead. The war has already been won. Satan knows his fate, but he wants us Christians to be ineffective, and he wants to prevent as many people from going to heaven as possible.

Jesus told us in Matthew 28:18, "All authority have been given to me in heaven and on earth." We now have the privilege of having an ongoing relationship with God. We are saved by grace, but Matthew 28:18 is not just about our salvation; it is also about our day-to-day victories over the enemy, which, cumulatively, result in a victorious life in Christ.

Let us examine the three grounds of spiritual battles: The Spiritual realm, the world, and the struggle within ourselves. We will review and discuss what the Bible says regarding these areas and we will find out how to use the scriptures in our personal lives to claim victory in these battles. It begins with learning the reality of God's Word and dispelling the lies of the enemy.

※ ※ ※

5. PRAYER FOR SPIRITUAL WARFARE

It's a good idea to start your battle against the enemy with a prayer. Here's one you might want to use as a model.

Father God, we humbly come to you, confessing that we are sinners saved by your grace. Please forgive us, Lord, in the Mighty name of Jesus for any sins we have committed. We can sense the dark spirit of the enemy. We acknowledge that he is at work trying to defeat us. He never gives up.

We need your supernatural power, Lord, to give us the victory and help us to never give in to the enemy. Physical strength will not help us; your Word says our weapons are not like earthly weapons. As believers our weapons are powerful, able to demolish the strongholds of the enemy. Through your mighty name and your blood, Jesus, we ask you to confuse Satan and thwart his efforts to hinder us. Help us to not become discouraged or to surrender when we are tested by the enemy.

When we are weak, you are strong. You are our only source of help. We cannot win this battle without you. Teach us to pray and trust you to tear down those strongholds that the enemy would construct to make us ineffective for the kingdom of God. Guard us against the isolation that leaves us exposed and vulnerable. We thank you Jesus for victory over the enemy through your death and resurrection. But, like a bad penny, our enemy keeps whispering lies, twisting reality, and appealing to our pride. He never gives up. But neither do you, Lord. And the devil is no match for you.

We are exposing Satan and his demons for what they are: liars. Through your precious name and your blood, Jesus, we accept as true your Word. That truth resides in us. Your Word and our prayers, Lord, are our secret weapons. The knowledge that we belong to you fills us with a powerful, God-given confidence. We are clothed in your spiritual armor. Help us to use that armor to defend ourselves and others from the enemy's attacks. Thank you for reminding us that you are always with us, in whatever we face. Thank you for the victory. We believe this prayer will not fall on deaf ears. In Jesus' name, Amen

✻ ✻ ✻

6. A PRAYER FOR COVER AGAINST EVIL

Evil is a difficult word to understand, but your Word defines it well. We ask for your protection against those who call good evil and evil good. Guard us against those who scheme against righteousness and from those who twist the truth to accomplish their evil intent. May your angels guard us. Eradicate fear and fight against the dark, spiritual forces we cannot see. Protect us against every imagination and thought that the enemy tries to use to exalt itself over us.

You dealt our spiritual enemy a fatal blow on Calvary. While evil still exists in this fallen world, your mighty name gives us the victory. While malicious actions may disturb us, we are clothed in the full armor of God. You will mete out justice in your time for all the harm done to your children. Until then, we stay in your presence, aligned with your purpose. We look to you as our Supreme Commander and Protector. Help us to resist temptation, and deliver us from all evil, Lord. You are the Mighty One, the one who will ultimately be victorious against all evil. With you Father, Son, and the Holy Spirit, we are safe. We count it all done, in Jesus' name amen.

A PRAYER TO PROTECT AGAINST SPIRITUAL ATTACKS

Lord, we want to say thank you for delivering us from ourselves and from this world. We know that the enemy would not be fighting so hard against us if we were not making a difference for your Kingdom. He would not be attacking us so relentlessly if he did not think we were a threat to his kingdom. Remind us today, Lord, that the battle belongs to you, and whatever we are up against will be taken down by your mighty hand. Please help us to trust you more, so that we don't spin our wheels, or try to fight in our own strength. Forgive us for the days we have neglected to align our hearts with you. Fill us with of your Holy Spirit. Give us strength to stand up to the enemy. Put the breastplate of righteousness on us. Help us to keep praising you as we face the enemy. Fill us with your wisdom and discernment, so that we can stand firm against his schemes. Thank you, Father for the constant reminders of your presence. In Jesus' name, amen.

PRAYER FOR COVER FROM THE WILES OF THE DEVIL

Ephesians 6:10-12 (KJV) says, "Finally, my brethren, be strong in the Lord, and the power of his might. Put on the whole armor of God that ye may be able to stand against the wiles of the devil. For we wrestle not against flesh and blood, but against principalities, against powers, against the rulers of the darkness of this world, against spiritual wickedness in high places."

The steps to equip the church to face the wiles of the devil, are the following:

- ❖ **Be strong in the Lord.**
  To be strong in the Lord is to deepen your conviction. To be strong in the Lord is to remind yourself why you are believing in and following him.
- ❖ **Be strong within His strength.**
  You will receive power after the Holy Spirit falls on you. You will receive strength as soon as you accept and are aligned with the Holy Spirit. The more you stay aligned with him, the more he empowers you. The Holy Spirit was given to us for our teaching, direction, and empowerment. He is the Spirit of Power and Might. When He comes in like a mighty rushing wind, he empowers and strengthens us.

- ❖ **Put on the entire armor of God.**

  We are to put on the entire armor of God. We are to be fully dressed for combat. God will not dress you; he wants you to dress yourself. We as Christians need to believe, do what is right, spread the Gospel, confess Christ to others , and read the Word of God. Most of these actions are our decisions. God will not do them for us, but He will bless us once we make the decision, and step out in faith.
- ❖ **Watch and pray with all perseverance for all the saints and ministers.**

Never stop praying, never stop watching. Pray, pray, and then pray some more; be constantly vigilant. Find time to watch and pray. Prayer is our main weapon against the enemy.

❋ ❋ ❋

7. HOW TO HAVE A PERSONAL CHRISTIAN DEVOTION

Devotions are an excellent way to meet up with God. Your devotion may be a quiet time that you spend praying, reading God's Word, praising, worshipping, and reflecting on your relationship with Him. You could also sing hymns, meditate, or write in a journal. If you set aside time every day to open your heart to God, you will find that this time becomes an essential part of our spiritual life.

Here are a few pointers to ensure an effective devotion time:

- **Find a place that is quiet and free from distractions.**

Ideally, to focus on God's Word you should not be in a noisy environment. Pick a quiet spot where you will feel comfortable. Turn off the TV, radio, or anything else that may distract you.

Psalm 46:10 says, "Be still, and know that I am God." If you are in a quiet environment, it is easier to get into His presence.

- **Open your devotion with prayer.**

Start your devotion time with a prayer to ask God to share his wisdom with you.

The Bible says in James 4:8, "Draw near to God and He will draw near to you." By reaching out to God at the start of our devotion, you will be more likely to feel His presence.

You could pray something like, "Dear God, please help me to understand your message today. Help me through your Holy Spirit to understand your word as I read it, and help me to make the right decisions throughout the day today."

- **During your devotion, read a verse from the Bible.**

One of the ways that God speaks to us is through his Word. There is no one way to read the Bible. It is, however, helpful to read a passage of Scripture in its context by reading the entire chapter. You can read the Bible straight through from Genesis to Revelation, or you can follow a Bible reading plan.

Highlight or underline verses that speak directly to you. When you reread that passage, it will serve as a reminder of a time when God talked to you personally.

You can supplement your devotional Bible reading with the reading of devotional books. There are devotionals written specifically for students, mothers, husbands, and other groups. You can also find daily devotionals online.

- **Reflect on what you read and how it applies to your own life**.

After reading a passage of Scripture, pause and meditate on its meaning. Think of how the passage relates to your life and your relationship with God.

If you are reading the tale of Jonah, for example, do not just imagine a human trapped inside a whale's belly. Consider how it feels to be in a hopeless position, and think of a time when you were in a similar situation. At that time, you probably felt like Jonah. Think of how God brought you out of that situation, as He brought Jonah out of the whale's belly.

You do not need to stop meditating on God's Word just because your devotion is over! If you memorize Scriptures, you can recall them up throughout your day.

- **Keep a journal to create a record of your spiritual journey.**

While you do not need to keep a journal, it often helps in organizing your thoughts, and it can provide a way for you to track your spiritual growth over time. Record your thoughts on what you are reading, prayers for yourself, favorite Bible verses, etc.

As with any journal, it's highly personal and does not need to follow any particular format.

- **If you prefer to worship this way, sing a hymn.**

Try singing hymns during your devotion routine if you find that this hymns helps you feel closer to God. "Sing to Him, sing praises to Him, say of all His wondrous works!" Psalm 105:2. Singing will help you express your love for God while also quieting your Spirit.

Remember that you are singing as a form of worship, not to impress anyone. It's normal to feel a bit self-conscious initially.

- **Close your devotion with prayer.**

Prayer is a good way to end your devotion. Pray about whatever is on your heart that day—you might want to praise God, ask Him to assist you with a problem you are facing, or pray for others.

In 1 Thessalonians 5:17, the Bible tells us to "Pray without ceasing." This means that you should constantly keep God in your thoughts, not just during your daily devotional time. But this does not take the place of setting aside time for more specific, intentional prayers.

- **Put aside the same time every day.**

In order for your devotions to be effective, it's important to be consistent. It helps to schedule your devotions for the same time every day. Pick a time and treat it like an important appointment, which it is. Don't schedule anything else during that time.

Many people like to start the day off with their devotion. Others prefer to have their devotion in the evening before bed, to reflect on everything that happened during the day. Find the time that works best for you.

Your devotion does not need to be long—start by setting aside 10-15 minutes each day. It may grow in length from there.

It's okay to be flexible. If you can't avoid a conflict with another appointment, then reschedule your time with God for that day. If you have to miss a day, just pick up where you left off previously.

- **Ask your family to respect your quiet time.**

If you live with other people, they might unintentionally interrupt you during your devotion. Let them know that you are spending some time every day with the Lord, and you would appreciate it if they left you alone during this time.

You could say something like, "Hey kids, I going to start doing a devotion every day at six in the morning. Can you keep the noise down until I am finished having my time with God?"

***

8. HOW ARE YOU INVOLVED IN SPIRITUAL WARFARE?

Spiritual warfare appears to be a battle between God and His enemies. What is *our* place in this battle?

If we have chosen to let God be Lord of our life, then we have asked Him to be head of *all things* in our life. But it's not easy or natural for us to turn over complete control of our lives to the Father. We struggle with this.

It might seem to you that there is a battle going on in your mind. Do you have days like this? Do you ever struggle with your faith? This is natural. The enemy Satan exploits these doubts in our minds.

The world and spiritual warfare

Society and culture influence us to act in certain ways. Some elements of society or culture can point us toward Jesus, some are neutral, and some directly conflict with our ability to follow Jesus and maintain a robust relationship with him.

Physical appearance, personal achievement, and independence are all valued in our Western culture. The world encourages us to place these things above God.

"For everything within the world-the lust of the flesh, the lust of the eyes, and therefore the pride of life come not from the Father but from evil on this world."

(1 John 2:16, NIV)

❋ ❋ ❋

9. FIGHTING THE SPIRITUAL BATTLE AS JESUS DID

Jesus faced spiritual warfare in various forms during his ministry on earth. The devil tested him for 40 days in wilderness (Luke 4: 1-13). He was criticized, falsely accused of many things, and verbally harassed by people who did not like what he was saying.

It is important to remember that Jesus, while he was on the earth, was a human being. He was subject to all of the temptations we face.

But he never lost a spiritual fight. His false arrest and crucifixion, which the world would view as his greatest failures, were ultimately his greatest triumphs. This was all part of God's plan. So, what can we learn from the life of Jesus on the subject of prayer in spiritual warfare?

How Jesus Fasted

The Bible teaches that fasting, combined with prayer, can help us to draw closer to God, and to better hear what he has to say to us.

Immediately before Jesus began his ministry, he fasted for forty days in the wilderness. The devil felt threatened when Jesus fasted and prayed, and tried to distract Jesus from his mission. Jesus viewed fasting as a weapon of spiritual warfare.

Fasting should be done wisely. You might want to check with your doctor before starting a lengthy fast. And you should never go without water during a fast. Learn more about this aspect of spiritual warfare by exploring the types of fasts for different trials in life.

The 7 Types of Christian Fasting: Which one is Right for You?

- ❖ Partial Fasting

- ❖ The Daniel Fast
- ❖ Complete Fasting
- ❖ Sexual Fasting
- ❖ Corporate Fasting
- ❖ Soul Fasting

❋ ❋ ❋

10. HOW TO PREPARE FOR SPIRITUAL WARFARE

The Bible often describes the Christian life using terms of war. This is where we get the term "spiritual warfare." Being a disciple of Christ means an ongoing struggle of putting God first in our lives. To be successful in this spiritual warfare, we of course need to acknowledge that we have an adversary, the devil.

2 Corinthians 10:3-4 (NIV) says, "For though we live in the world, we do not wage war as the world does. The weapons we fight with are not the weapons of the world. On the contrary, they have divine power to demolish strongholds."

The spiritual realm is real, and Christians must find out how to fight the battle taking place there. The good news is that God gives us the weapons we need to defend ourselves in this spiritual battle. We have hope, because he has already defeated the devil through the death and resurrection of Jesus Christ. We have the power and strength of the Holy Spirit fighting for us.

The Breastplate of Righteousness

To put on the breastplate of righteousness means to wear the righteousness that Jesus purchased for us when he died on the cross. It does not mean we try to protect ourselves against Satan with our own righteousness. We are not justified through our own actions. We merely claim by faith God's righteousness made available to us through Jesus' work on the cross.

When we live according to God's will, and say no to sin, we actively live out the righteousness we have as followers of Jesus Christ. Righteousness is something we are given by God at the time of salvation, but it's also something that we grow into. We are covered in Christ's righteousness that declares us innocent before God, and his righteousness allows us to grow in our own obedience. The

Holy Spirit matures us day by day.

The Sword of the Spirit

The sword of the Spirit is God's Word, the Bible. This is the only piece of our spiritual equipment designed for offensive use. In the first Century, the sword was a powerful tool for the infantry soldier. It was designed to incapacitate the enemy efficiently and quickly. We need this weapon against our spiritual enemy.

Try praying the following Bible verses when you are engaged in combat with the enemy, this world, the flesh, or the devil. You can insert our own name or the name of somebody you are praying for to personalize the verse.

2 Corinthians 10:3-5 (NIV)

"For though we live in the world, we do not wage war as the world does. The weapons we fight with are not the weapons of the world. On the contrary, they have divine power to demolish strongholds. We demolish arguments and every pretension that sets itself up against the knowledge of God, and we take captive every thought to make it obedient to Christ."

Isaiah 54:17 (NIV)

"'No weapon forged against you will prevail, and you will refute every tongue that accuses you. This is the heritage of the servants of the LORD, and this is their vindication from me,' declares the LORD."

John 8:32 (NIV)

"Then you will know the truth, and the truth will set you free."

1 Peter 5:7 (NIV)

"Cast all of your anxiety on Him because He cares for you."

John 15:7 (NIV)

"If you remain in Me and My words remain in you, ask whatever you wish, and it will be done for you."

✻ ✻ ✻

11. SEASONED BELIEVERS

People who have been in the faith for years can act as mentors to less mature believers, and give them solid, Bible-based advice. Mature Christians will encourage us to read the Bible for ourselves and not just rely on what they say. Knowing the Bible yourself will keep you from being deceived or misled, or becoming a member of a cult. As John 8:32 says, "You shall know the truth, and the truth shall set you free."

John 17:17 says, "Thy word is truth." Many people young in the faith rely on someone else to lead them into all truth. They give credence to man's word more than to God's Word. But there's no substitute for reading the Bible yourself. 2 Timothy 2:15 (KJV) says, "Study to shew thyself approved unto God, a workman that needeth not to be ashamed, rightly dividing the Word of truth."

In Acts 17, the people of Berea were excited about receiving the Word of God from Paul and Silas. They received the Word with readiness of mind, and they searched the Scriptures daily to see if the things they were told were true. Acts 17:11 says of the Bereans, "These were more fair-minded than those in Thessalonica, in that they received the word with all readiness, and searched the Scriptures daily *to find out* whether these things were so."

It is important that Christians mature in the faith have patience and compassion for newer believers, and resist the temptation to feel superior to them. The younger generation needs guidance and wisdom from those who have a few years of experience under their belts.

Psalm 91: 7 says, "A thousand may fall at your side,
And ten thousand at your right hand; *But* it shall not come near you."

"It's important that we mature Christians act as mentors to the next generation of Christians, these new recruits in the army against the enemy. These young believers do not have our wisdom, but they have the energy and enthusiasm that we may lack, and they can gain wisdom with our help. Those veterans of spiritual warfare can provide the training that will ensure victory against Satan for the new generation of believers. Look around you: How can you be of service to newer believers? How can you help those who have a heart to serve God, yet are not yet equipped to do so?

There needs to be a connection between the old and the new generation, like a relay runner passing a baton. What the older generation may feel ill-equipped to do because they were brought up in a different culture, the newer, younger generation will rise to the occasion to accomplish. We need to be flexible enough to recognize the new direction God is taking his church. Don't get too comfortable in your old ways of thinking, even if they worked for you in the past.

God is doing something new, which will shake up the establishment in every area of our society, as he is equipping and empowering new, up-and-coming leaders. Don't worry about How God is going to accomplish this. Just focus on who it is that is doing it. If you ask him, God will reveal to you which individuals or groups he wants you to mentor.

To those of us in the older generation, allow the younger generation to take over and lead. They, not us, were born for this hour.

✽ ✽ ✽

12. SPIRITUAL WARFARE FOR EACH BELIEVER

The term spiritual warfare sometimes conjures images of angels and demons fighting it out in the skies.

That's not exactly what spiritual warfare is about. It is a real battle, albeit unseen, between the forces of evil lead be Satan, and the forces of good, lead by God. We as Christians are on the side of good. Whether we like it or not, we are in this battle. We can try to engage in this battle using our own strength and strategy, or we can do it according to the Bible.

Some believers, in their engagement of the enemy, focus almost exclusively on the demon realm, binding evil spirits, driving away demons, and demolishing the demon's stronghold.

However, this focus may not be the most effective way to combat the enemy. It can lead us into battles that we were not designed to fight, and keep us from achieving a spiritual breakthrough as taught by the Bible. It can dissipate our energy and resources by engaging in a battle whose victory would not greatly benefit us.

The New Testament and the Old Testament book of Daniel show us how we should engage in this spiritual warfare.

In the Gospels, Jesus and his disciples addressed directly the demons that were possessing or oppressing a person. These were "embodied" demonic spirits, which are not the same as the evil forces that can oppress an entire geographic region on the earth. So, there is a clear distinction between demons inhabiting a person and demonic forces that have influence over an entire region.

Ephesians 6:12 (NKJV) says, "For we do not wrestle against flesh and blood, but against principalities, against powers, against the rulers of the darkness of this age, against spiritual *hosts* of wickedness in the heavenly *places.*" This, however, does not refer to the fighting of demons directly. It is talking about battling demonic forces that are oppressing an entire geographical area on the earth.

There are exceptions to this spiritual rule, when the Holy Spirit prompts us to deal directly with the enemy, but this is not the norm we see in Scripture.

If we follow the biblical model, we should pray to the Father for a spiritual breakthrough over a geographical area, whether that be a city, state or nation. The Lord wants his people to get involved in this battle. He does hear and answer our prayers.

As we read in the ninth and tenth chapters of the book of Daniel, the prophet was able to defeat the demonic force ruling over Persia by fasting and praying, and by focusing on Yahweh, the God of Israel, not on the evil force itself.

Daniel, while he was praying and fasting, wasn't even aware of the spiritual battle that was being waged until an angel informed him of it. This angel also revealed to Daniel what was going to happen to Israel, and the future of the world. Daniel focused on God through prayer and fasting, and God heard his prayers and acted. It can be the same for us if we are willing to fast and pray.

You may be praying for a breakthrough in the city where you live. This story from the book of Daniel shows you how to go about it.

As believers, we can defeat the enemy by worshipping God and breaking agreement with the enemy. We can bring about justice to the oppressed, knowing that our heavenly Father will pour out His blessing, and deliver us from spiritual darkness.

✳ ✳ ✳

13. SIX SPIRITUAL SEASONS OF LIFE

If you looked at your life, what season of life would you say you are currently in? Are you in a dry season, a waiting-for-something season, a grinding season, a tests-and-trials-at-nearly-every-turn season, or a spiritual warfare season? There are many more possibilities. Maybe you are enjoying a happy season, and all is well with you and your family. Sometimes it is difficult to recognize the season of life we are in, and sometimes it is even harder to understand the way to live fully in Christ during that season.

In nature, seasons don't last forever. There is winter, spring, summer, and fall. Like the seasons in nature, our spiritual seasons change too.

The Bible tells us in Ecclesiastes 3:1, "For everything, there's a season." And in Ecclesiastes 3:11 it says, "[God] has made everything beautiful in its time."

Step one is to develop a sense to recognize which season you are in. Here are six seasons in a believer's life. Which one describes your current life?

1. The Silent Season

This is a difficult season to endure. When God is silent, you cannot hear his presence as much as you used to. During this season, God seems distant. I have lived through this season at various times of my life, so I understand how hard this one can be. For Christians, the spiritual drought season can seem unbearable. In this season, your life experience is not in line with what you recognize to be true about God. If God guides his children, why can't I feel it? If he cares, why don't I think it?

I believe the key to getting through this challenging season is: (1) Realize that you simply are in it, and (2) Press through it – draw near to God, in spite of how distant he feels. Do not allow yourself to dry up spiritually. Continue reading his Word and praying. He is still there, and he still hears you, even though you don't hear him. He has not left.

2. The Waiting Season

Let me start this on by saying, waiting is not easy. If you are there now and you're getting tired of waiting, take heart.

Psalm 37:7 says, "Rest in the Lord, and wait patiently for him."

Whether you are waiting for a godly spouse, for a difficult situation to pass, or for God to fulfill a promise, the waiting season can range from quite annoying to almost unbearable.

We know from the story of Joseph when he was unjustly thrown into an Egyptian prison, that God uses this season for his glory and our good. We know from Abraham's story in Genesis that the waiting period might last a while. We also know from Hannah's story that pouring your heart out to God and waiting on him pays off in the long run.

In the waiting season, believe that God is developing you. He chips away what is not needed in your life. He is preparing you for your future, so let him do his work on you.

3. The Milling Season

Also known as the busy season, this is the season where you say, "I do not have enough time to get everything done!" Sometimes we have big projects or little people that need more of our time than in other seasons. I am in this season as I write this.

Our culture places value on busyness, but it is not something that Christians should pursue. If you find yourself in this season, pursue God. The key to succeeding during this time is to seek God for direction the instant you get out of bed in the morning. Recognize and organize what must get done, then wade through those priorities. Prioritizing your daily activities will help ease the stress.

"In his hand are the depths of the world, and therefore the mountain peaks belong to him," Psalm 95:4.

The whole world does not rest in your hands – it rests in God's hands. Psalm 95:4 says, "In his hand are the depths of the world, and therefore the mountain peaks belong to him."

Pace yourself and your tasks. Breathe. Pray. Take a lunch break. Then continue in your grind and press through with the strength God gives you. Believe the Holy Spirit will guide and assist you.

4. The Tests & Trials Season

If you are experiencing adversity during this season, know that God is with you in the midst of it all. He is at work, whether you realize it or not. I do know it is hard when you are in the midst of this season; you might not even understand what you are going through, or why. However, I would like to encourage you that God knows, and in due time, all is going to be revealed. In the meantime, do not become discouraged in doing good.

"Let us not become weary in doing good, for in due season we shall reap, if we do not lose heart," Galatians 6:9.

If you would like comfort, let God comfort you. If you need strength beyond your own strength, let him strengthen you. If you would like wisdom, ask. James 1:5 promises that God will give wisdom to those who ask. Allow God to be God. He doesn't need your help. Allow Him to do the supernatural work that only he can do. Allow him to strengthen and increase your faith during this season of hardship or affliction.

5. The Spiritual Warfare Season

If you are currently in this season of spiritual warfare, take heart. If you are spiritually attacked, that shows that you are doing something right that Satan does not like. If you are walking faithfully, the enemy will wage war against you. Expect it. This comes with being a Christian. Do not be afraid. Remember the story of Job: God is in complete control.

This is the great thing about being a child of God: He fights for us. We only lean into him and believe him by praying and reading his Word. He will look out for us.

This is not a natural battle against flesh and blood.

"For our struggle is not against flesh and blood, but against the rulers, against the authorities, against the powers of this dark world and against the spiritual forces of evil within the heavenly realms," Ephesians 6:12.

We must gird ourselves with all of our spiritual armor.

"Therefore, put on the full armor of God so that when the day of evil comes, you may be able to stand your ground, and after you have done everything, to stand. Stand firm then, with the belt of truth buckled around your waist, with the breastplate of righteousness in place, and with your feet fitted with the readiness that comes from the gospel of peace. In addition to all this, take up the shield of faith, with which you can extinguish all the flaming arrows of the evil one. Take the helmet of salvation and the sword of the Spirit, which is the Word of God," Ephesians 6:13-17.

6. The Happy Season

"Is anyone among you in trouble? Let them pray. Is anyone happy? Let them sing songs of praise," James 5:13.

Maybe you're a newlywed, or your kids are at the age where they are giving you a lot of pleasure. Perhaps you are killing it at work. Or you are reading the Bible and it is making sense to you as never before. This is the fun season – the happy season. But just because it's a fun season, that doesn't mean you don't have a job to do: Praise the Lord! Praising God is something Christians should do in every season because our hearts need it, and because God deserves it.

❊ ❊ ❊

14. A PRAYER FOR WHEN ENEMIES STRIKE

O Lord our God, you have existed throughout eternity; you are great in compassion as you are in power; because of your mercy, sent your son to become one of us that we might have forgiveness of sins and salvation. Hear us now and have mercy on us. We ask that you, master of all, hear our requests.

We acknowledge your great love for your creation and your goodness towards us. We ask that you not hide your face from us. Have mercy on us. Show us the way to rise above both our visible and invisible enemies. Place in us your power; hold us in your right hand; keep us under the protection of your wings; help us to love one another, and grant us the peace that comes only from you. Instill in us a fear and respect for you, that your holy name may be glorified in us. On you alone we have placed our hopes, and to you, be the glory. In Jesus' name, amen.

✳ ✳ ✳

15. EIGHT FUNCTIONS OF THE HOLY SPIRIT, AS TAUGHT BY JESUS

1. He Dwells in us

John 14:17: Even the Spirit of truth; whom the world cannot receive, because it sees Him not, neither knows Him: but you know Him; for He dwells with you and shall be in you.

This dwelling in us is the baptism of the Holy Spirit.

2. He Teaches us all things

John 14:26: But the Comforter, who is the Holy Spirit, whom the Father will send in My name, He shall teach you all things and bring all things to your remembrance, whatsoever I have said unto you.

3. He Testifies of Jesus Christ

John 15:26: But when the Comforter has come, whom I will send unto you from the Father, even the Spirit of truth, who proceeds from the Father, He shall testify of me.

4. He Convicts the world of sin, righteousness, and judgment

John 16:8: And when he has come, he will reprove the world of sin, and of righteousness, and of judgment.

John 16:9: Of sin, because they believe not on me.

John 16:10: Of righteousness, because I go to my Father, and ye see me no more.

John 16:11: Of judgment, because the prince of this world is judged.

5. He guides us in all truth

John 16:13: However, when He, the Spirit of truth, is come, He will guide you into all truth: for He shall not speak of Himself; but whatsoever He shall hear, that shall He speak.

6. He tells us of things to come

… and he will show you things to come (John 16:13)

John 16:14-15: He will glorify Me, for He will take of what is Mine and declare it to you. All things that the Father has are Mine. Therefore I said that He will take of Mine and declare it to you.

How do we see the future? – The future is revealed in the Word of God, and it is the Holy Spirit dwelling in us that helps us to understand his Word.

7. He glorifies Jesus

In John 16:14, Jesus says, "He shall glorify me."

8. He, the Holy Spirit, speaks.

John 16:13: However, when He, the Spirit of truth, is come, He will guide you into all truth: for He shall not speak of Himself; but whatsoever He shall hear, that shall He speak.

Father, I thank you for this day, and I ask that this book deliver and heal your people. Lord I pray that the reading and teaching of this book pierce the heart of those who read it, and place hot coals on the head of our enemies.

I pray that your Word reaches the masses. I speak with all power and authority that the enemy's stronghold be broken. Your Word is true, your love and kindness towards us are real, your blood has the power to shake up the foundations of this world. We are more than conquerors through Christ Jesus, who gives us strength to trample over the devil and walk in Spirit and in truth. I pray that people's lives, hearts, situations, and thought processes would shift after reading this book. Your son Jesus will rule this world someday. I thank your Holy Spirit for doing a new thing in your people. In Jesus' name amen.

VIRGINIA'S MESSAGE TO HER READERS

Satan is committed to preventing people from knowing God and trusting Him with their whole hearts and lives. Some believe that once you get saved, it is smooth sailing. That is far from the truth. Yes, you are protected by the Holy Spirit, and the enemy does not like that. When you were out in the world, the devil was not worried about you. But now that you are following Christ Jesus, you are on Satan's hit list. Your spiritual warfare journey has begun. This book will walk you through the stages of life that await you. With the Holy Trinity of God, you will come out of your battle on TOP.

ABOUT THE AUTHOR

Virginia A.lewis

Virginia A Lewis is a God-fearing woman; she was raised in the church her whole life. Ms. Lewis comes from a lineage of Pastors, Bishops, and Elders. Virginia built her foundation of the Word of God and love for Jesus Christ from her grandfather, the late Elder Curtis O. Lewis. Virginia accepted Jesus Christ as her Lord and Savior at a young age. She started studying Spiritual Warfare fifteen years ago, when she met her spiritual mother, Crystal. Virginia has been through the storm and the rain. Crystal challenged Virginia to dig deep into God's Word to learn who she is, and how to stand up against the attacks of Satan. Spiritual warfare has been Virginia's Mission ever since. She believes all men and women of God need to know how to stand up and fight the devil, because the devil sure knows how to fight you.

Virginia's Message to Her Readers

Satan is committed to preventing people from knowing God and trusting Him with their whole hearts and lives. Some believe that once you get saved, it is smooth sailing. That is far from the truth. Yes, you are protected by the Holy Spirit, and the enemy does not like that. When you were out in the world, the devil was not worried about you. But now that you are following Christ Jesus, you are on Satan's hit list. Your spiritual warfare journey has begun. This book will walk you through the stages of life that await you. With the Holy Trinity of God, you will come out of your battle on TOP.

Made in the USA
Middletown, DE
10 May 2022